THE
SAN DIEGO
CHARGERS

Published by Creative Education, Inc., 123 South Broad Street, Mankato, Minnesota
56001

Library of Congress Catalog Card No.: 85-72629

ISBN: 0-88682-047-2

THE
SAN DIEGO
CHARGERS

JAMES R. ROTHAUS

CREATIVE EDUCATION

An intense man with a genius for organizing, Sid Gillman was easily the best coach in the newborn American Football League.

SAN DIEGO
LIGHTNING

The lightning bolts on their shoulders are the perfect symbol for the San Diego Chargers and especially for the great quarterbacks who have led this team's relentless aerial attack over the past three decades.

Like Thor, the mythical Norse god of thunder, quarterbacks Jack Kemp, Tobin Rote, John Hadl, Danny Fouts and others have zapped the rest of the league by unleashing the lightning in their powerful throwing arms.

"It's always a little scary playing against San Diego," complained rugged Seattle Seahawk linebacker Michael Jackson after a hard-fought loss to the Chargers back in 1983. "They have this long tradition of being an explosive passing team, and Fouts is kind of the essence of that tradition.

"He goes back in the pocket and you say to yourself, 'There's just no way he's going to get this pass off.' And the next thing you know, he whistles one through everyone's arms and it just threads its way out there into some receiver's hands. It's like he's got the ball all wired up to some sort of weird homing device."

When Dan Fouts hears this kind of compliment, he feels uncomfortable. His close friends say that Danny seldom reads a newspaper or magazine article about himself. It it's an article about the team, that's fine, he'll read it. But if it's a story about the individual achievements of Dan Fouts, he'll usually shake his head and turn the page.

"I know it's been said before," explains Fouts in that quiet, friendly way of his, "but football is a team game. If the linemen don't protect me, if the receivers don't get clear for me, if the running backs don't execute properly. . .heck, I'd just be another quarterback in the dust. So, if you're going to write a book, tell the story of the entire San Diego team and organization."

Good suggestion, Mr. Fouts. Here, then, is the story of the great Charger tradition, from day-one.

IT ALL BEGAN
IN 1960

The critics laughed and called it the "Mickey Mouse League." The year was 1960, and the announcement had recently gone out that a new group of pro football teams had banded together to form the American Football League. There were eight teams in the league, and they intended to compete with the old, established NFL for fan support. According to the experts, the chances that the new AFL would survive were slim. . .and none.

The AFL players were not, after all, the cream of the crop. The truth is, most of them were NFL rejects, at least in the early days. So were the coaches. Few of them had ever been anything but assistant coaches in the NFL. One of the few exceptions was Sid Gillman.

Gillman had coached the Los Angeles Rams to a divisional title in his first year. The key to his success in L.A. had been the passing game. He knew it like no one

Ron Mix (74) rides shotgun for rusher Keith Lincoln in an early game. Mix was enshrined in Football's Hall of Fame in 1979. He was an eight-time All-League tackle, playing with the Chargers from 1960 through 1969.

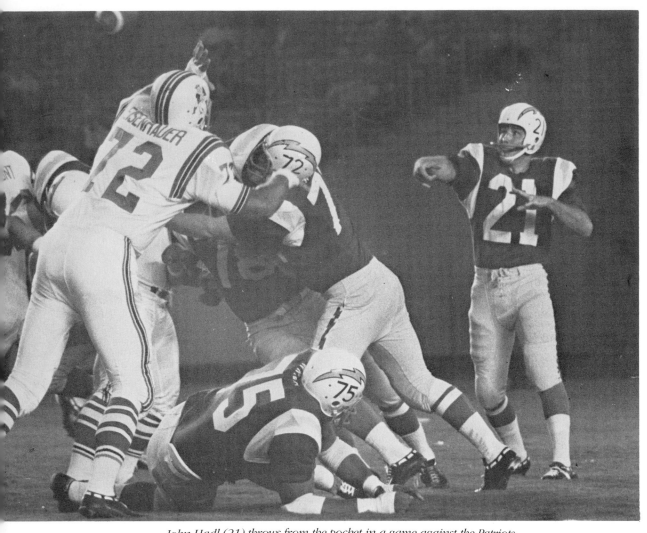

John Hadl (21) throws from the pocket in a game against the Patriots.

else. His teams were more than just winners, they were exciting to watch.

That made Gillman an extremely sought-after man when he left the Rams in 1959. Nearly every professional team, both in the AFL and NFL, wanted him as its coach. But it was millionaire Barron Hilton who snatched his services.

Less than six months earlier, Hilton had purchased the AFL franchise rights to Los Angeles. After signing Gillman, Hilton's team became an immediate favorite for the first AFL Championship, even though there were no players yet!

Even fans who sneered at the rest of the AFL had to admit that Hilton's team, named the Chargers, would probably be the equal of any NFL team. The reason was Gillman. He was years ahead of his time. He always had been.

Back in the 1940's, he had been one of the first to switch to a two-platoon system. He had diagrammed plays carefully, rather than making them up as the game went along. And he had designed pass-receiving routes long before post- and crossing-patterns had even been a consideration among the other NFL coaches.

A FAST START

Despite his previous success, Gillman had secret doubts about his first Charger team. They looked good in practice, but he wondered how they would react in a real game. It didn't take long to find out.

Did you know?

Coached by Sid Gillman, a West team featuring 11 Chargers defeated the East, 47-27, in the first AFL all-star game in 1962.

The 27,000 fans in the Los Angeles Coliseum for the Chargers' first preseason game had hardly settled into their seats, when halfback Paul Lowe scooped up the opening kickoff five yards deep in his own end zone. Lowe didn't hesitate to run it out. He had speed to burn. In the blink of an eye he was gone, screaming down the sideline 105 yards for the touchdown. The Chargers were on their way!

Behind Lowe and quarterback Jack Kemp, the Chargers streaked to the AFL Western Division crown with a 10-4 record that first season. They then met the Houston Oilers in a hard-fought contest for the AFL Championship.

Los Angeles opened an early 6-0 lead with two field goals by "Toeless" Ben Agajanian, who had four toes missing on his kicking foot. But Houston slowly crept back, taking a slim 17-16 lead into the fourth quarter. Twice Kemp directed the Chargers to the Oilers' goal line, only to come up short. Finally, Houston put Los Angeles out of its misery with a long touchdown pass. The final score was 24-16, Houston.

MOVING SOUTH
TO SAN DIEGO

Despite their good showing on the field, the first-year Chargers had been losers at the box office. Most of the Los Angeles gridiron fans were loyal to just one team—the L.A. Rams of the NFL. Down south in San Diego, however, the city was starving for pro football. It seemed only natural that the Chargers should oblige

John Hadl throws and Keith Lincoln blocks in a 1964 contest against Oakland.

Lance Alworth skips away from a ball-hungry Houston Oiler.

them. In 1961, the L.A. Chargers became the San Diego Chargers.

Sure enough, when the Chargers played their first game at San Diego's Balboa Stadium, a big crowd was on hand to see their new team get revenge on Houston, 27-14. The Chargers had brought along a bumper crop of rookies signed by Gillman during the off-season. Former college stars Earl Faison, Keith Lincoln and Ernie Ladd had all been courted by the NFL. But Coach Gillman, a great salesman, was able to lure them away. Together with Lowe, Kemp and Ron Mix, a standout tackle, the San Diego Chargers stormed to a 12-2 mark in '61 and another Western Division title.

For the second year in a row, the Chargers met Houston for the league crown. And once again they bowed, 10-3.

The next season, 1962, promised to be different. Not only had the Chargers drafted a brilliant young quarterback by the name of John Hadl, but they had also acquired Lance Alworth, a shifty flanker, in a trade. It was considered a high-rev offense with Hadl's passing, Alworth's catching and the combination running of Lincoln and Lowe. But everything backfired. Hadl was still too young and inexperienced. Alworth and Lowe were lost to injury. The result was a disappointing 4-10 record.

To help ease the pressure on Hadl, Gillman signed veteran QB Tobin Rote for 1963. With Alworth and Lowe healthy again, the season got off to a hard-chargin' start.

San Diego stacked victory upon victory, winning five in a row to start the season. The record rose to 7-1 when Rote passed for 369 yards in a win over the New York Jets. Victories over arch-rival Houston followed.

Late in the season, when Rote was experiencing arm trouble, Gillman handed the reins back to Hadl. The young QB responded with a five-TD effort in a big 47-23 victory over Denver for the division championship.

San Diego went forward into the league title game in Boston as the underdog. But after the first period, in which the Chargers scored three touchdowns, the Patriots saw the handwriting on the wall. The scores came on a run by Rote, a 67-yard gallop by Lincoln and a 58-yard scoring sprint by Lowe.

The lead swelled from 31-10 at half-time to 51-10 by midway through the final quarter. Lincoln was awarded the game ball for compiling an amazing 206 yards on the ground. Meanwhile, Hadl and Rote had combined for 285 yards through the air.

RECHARGING THE CHARGERS

Winning division titles got to be old-hat for the Chargers in the early and mid-Sixties. In the first six years of the AFL's existence, San Diego won five Western crowns and appeared in five championship games, winning one. It's easy to see why they were so dominant; the roster was loaded with all-stars.

First, you had Hadl, one of the purest passers football has ever known. He was fearless in the face of the rush, and his throwing arm was jam-packed with power. Running underneath Hadl's towering spirals was Lance Alworth, the most explosive deep-threat in either league in those days.

*On September 30, 1973, John Unitas completed a 30-yard pass to Mike
Garrett in a game against Cincinnati— becoming the first man in NFL
history to pass for 40,000 total yards. He was inducted into Football's
Hall of Fame in 1979.*

Charlie Joiner, here hauling in a touchdown pass in a game against Cincinnati, became one of the best outside receivers in the NFL.

When Hadl's arm got tired, Keith Lincoln and Paul Lowe were always ready to take the ball and run. On defense there was punt-return specialist Speedy Duncan, interception king Bud Whitehead, and All-Pro linemen Earl Faison and Ernie Ladd.

Yet, with all this talent, the Chargers fell short of a championship. In both 1964 and 1965, Buffalo beat San Diego for the league title. Sid Gillman was as perplexed as anyone. "Why can't we win the Big Game?" he asked.

Some blamed Gillman's coaching. Others pointed to the players, who were constantly asking for more money. In fact, Faison and Ladd actually left the team when they weren't granted raises. Overnight, it seemed, San Diego dropped from contention. As a result, fewer and fewer college stars elected to sign with the Chargers. It was a vicious cycle that eventually sent San Diego into a tailspin.

Mind you, the Chargers were still a respectable club. They managed four consecutive winning seasons in 1966-69. But their fans expected more than just victories, they wanted championships. Consequently, crowds began to decline as San Diego fell to third in the Western Division behind Oakland and Kansas City. At the time, it seemed silly for the Chargers to move into the spacious new San Diego Stadium with its 50,000 seats. Within 15 years, however, an additional 25,000 seats would not be enough to hold all the loyal Chargers fans!

The move to the new stadium in 1967, however, did little to help the team's performance. In the stadium dedication game, the Chargers lost to Detroit by the embarrassing score of 38-17.

By the way, it was now possible for AFL clubs such as

Did you know?

In the final game of the 1972 season, the Chargers' Mike Garrett gained 59 yards to finish with 1,031 yards and become the only pro player to gain 1,000 yards with two different teams. He had eclipsed the 1,000-mark with Kansas City in 1967.

the Chargers to meet teams like the NFL's Detroit Lions because of a peace treaty between the two leagues. As part of the merger, the two league champions would meet to settle the world title in the Super Bowl.

HADL LEADS
THE WAY

John Hadl wanted to play in a Super Bowl in the worst way. Though he already owned all the team passing records, he was not satisfied. "All the records are great," he said, "but San Diego fans deserve a championship."

Hadl did his best to deliver the title, sometimes single-handedly. His desperate—but effective—scoring strikes in the final minutes of a game became his trademark.

"I call him 'Cliff-hanger Hadl,'" joked Coach Gillman. "If a game goes down to the final minute, John is the best guy in the league at pulling something out of the hat."

Hadl wasn't a big man. In his prime, however, he stood head-and-shoulders above any other quarterback in the league. He passed for an astounding 3,400 yards and 27 touchdowns in 1968—far and away the best totals in either league.

With Hadl extending Gillman's wide-open offense to the limit, the Chargers became the AFL's highest-scoring team. The loss of Faison and Ladd took a heavy toll on the defense, however, and even Hadl couldn't score enough points to keep up with the opposition.

Meanwhile, Sid Gillman's patience was wearing thin.

With tackle Billy Shields holding off the opposition, quarterback James Harris prepares for aerial attack.

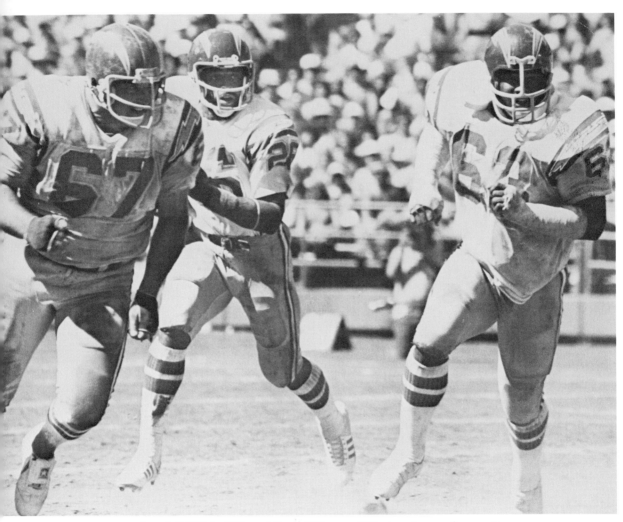

Guards Ed White (67) and Doug Wilkerson (63) clear the way for a gain by rusher Lydell Mitchell.

He had a constant case of the jitters. Eventually, a nervous ulcer forced him to step down midway through the 1969 campaign, leaving assistant Charlie Waller in charge.

Waller directed the club to four straight victories, but the Chargers narrowly missed the playoffs for the fourth straight season. In 1970, when regular inter-conference scheduling began, San Diego was outmanned by the NFL's "big boys." For the first time in seven years, the record sagged under the .500 mark to 5-6-3.

OUT WITH
THE OLD,
IN WITH
THE NEW

Sid Gillman came back as head coach in 1971, hoping to turn the team around. But things just weren't the same. Eugene Klein was now the majority owner. Alworth was gone, traded to Dallas. The running backs were no longer Lincoln and Lowe, but Mike Garrett and Jeff Queen. About the only holdover was John Hadl, who was now balding with age.

Klein and Gillman butted heads on a regular basis. By the end of the season it was obvious Gillman would have to leave.

Harland Svare, the team's general manager, took over Gillman's coaching duties. At first, Svare seemed to be just what the doctor ordered, having built several clubs into defensive powers earlier in his career. One of his previous assignments had been as defensive coach under

Charger tight end Greg McCrary became an instant hero in 1978. In this 1979 photo, he catches a touchdown pass in a game against Minnesota.

Big Louie Kelcher, beloved by San Diego fans, checked in at 6-foot-5 and 282 pounds. Here he puts the crunch on Houston's Fred Willis.

Talented Dan Fouts joined the Chargers in 1973 but did not become a starter until 1976. He was a holdout in 1977, not reporting until November 18; but then made up for lost time in a sizzling attack on Seattle, completing 19 of 26 throws for 199 yards and a touchdown.

the immortal Vince Lombardi at Green Bay!

Lombardi was known to be a hard-driving disciplinarian. He had little use for high-priced players who didn't produce. Svare added an interesting twist to Lombardi's philosophy. You see, Svare believed he could round up all the other teams' talented "undesirables" and mold them into disciplined winners in San Diego. It was a risky strategy, one that Lombardi probably would have sided against. But Svare was determined to bring in a whole new team, if necessary. Over the off-season, he made a record 21 trades in collecting his basket of talented bad apples.

There were the problem players, men like Duane Thomas, Walker Gillette, Jerry LeVias and Tim Rossovich. There were also players who had seen their better days—legends like Deacon Jones, John Mackey and the great Johnny Unitas. Together, this odd collection of "undesirables" added up to a disaster in 1972.

In 1973, matters got worse as Hadl was traded and the Chargers sank to 2-11-1. Svare, whose strategy had obviously failed, was later fired.

In came Tommy Prothro, a new coach with a completely different outlook and approach. Prothro didn't promise the world, he simply asked fans "to be patient. In time, we'll make you proud of the Chargers again."

Prothro was the exact opposite of Svare. He liked to recruit young, stable players and rebuild through the college draft. He had proven that theory as a top college coach at UCLA and again in the pros with the Los Angeles Rams. In two seasons with Los Angeles, Prothro had stocked the Rams with many excellent players but had failed to take them to playoffs.

Did you know?

Why do they call him "Air" Coryell? The year before Don Coryell took over as head coach of the Chargers the team set a record for fewest pass attempts in a game (7). Under Coryell the team then set a record for most pass attempts in a game (57).

Sadly, this was Tommy Prothro's fate at San Diego, too. He was a shrewd builder and an outstanding judge of talent. But for some reason, he couldn't translate those gifts into victories. Give credit to Prothro, however, for laying a solid foundation for the Chargers' later success.

During his four seasons at San Diego, Prothro drafted such future greats as Dan Fouts, Gary Johnson, Rickey Young, Louie Kelcher, Woodrow Lowe, Joe Washington and Fred Dean. He also obtained the likes of Don Woods and Charlie Joiner. But it took time for these talented, inexperienced players to gel. Despite Prothro's reminder to be patient, fans grew restless for success.

It was not until 1977 that the Chargers finally broke even at 7-7, ending seven years of frustration as a losing team. It also marked a new beginning for San Diego. Now the Chargers appeared ready to reclaim the Western Division crown.

A BOLT FROM
OUT OF THE BLUE

Prothro put the finishing touches on the '78 team by making two brilliant moves. First he drafted John Jefferson, a sleek, speedy wide-receiver from Arizona State. Then, in a summer trade with the Colts, he obtained multipurpose running back Lydell Mitchell, one of the NFL's premier offensive threats. With reliable QB James Harris triggering the attack, everything pointed to a great year. Even the cautious Coach Prothro suggested that the long wait might be over.

Number One Draft choice for 1978, John "JJ" Jefferson sparkled as a receiver in his rookie year.

Johnny Rodgers (20), kick-return specialist and wide receiver, squares off against Viking cornerback Nate Allen. He won the Heisman Trophy in 1972.

The Chargers cruised to an opening-day victory over Seattle, 24-20, behind a key interception by Gary "Big Hands" Johnson. However, the next three opponents would not be so kind.

The following week, Oakland scored on the last play of the game to break San Diego's heart, 21-20. A week later, Denver came from behind to clout the Chargers, 27-14. Then, in the sweltering 105-degree heat of their own stadium, the Chargers fell far and hard, this time to Green Bay, 24-3.

Fans jeered and booed Coach Prothro as he left the field. They felt betrayed. They had waited seven years for a winner. Now, just when the team had begun to show signs of improvement, the Chargers were sliding back into the cellar. Prothro loved the team too much to see it lose. One day after the Packer loss he resigned.

The players didn't know it at the time, but Prothro's replacement was already in town, ready to step in as soon as he received the nod from Klein. Like a flash from the past or a bolt from the blue, Don Coryell had resurfaced in San Diego.

Before he even set foot on the Chargers' practice field, Coryell was already a local legend. Earlier in his career, he had coached San Diego State University to a fantastic 104-19-2 record in 12 years. After that, he had moved up to the pros and helped guide the St. Louis Cardinals from the cellar to the playoffs in just two years. After a so-so 7-7 finish in 1977, however, Coryell had been released from the Cardinals. They may not have wanted him in St. Louis, but the folks back home were sure eager to have him back.

Coryell was known as a man who appealed to his

players' emotions. Fans were sure that he could spark a new charge in San Diego's battery. Unlike Prothro, Coach Coryell put the team through rugged, gut-wrenching workouts. No more Mr. Nice Guy! It was time to play hard-nosed football again.

Almost immediately, the Chargers burst back on the scene as a contender. In Coryell's first game back, only a lucky last-minute TD by New England gave the Patriots a 28-23 win. The next week against Denver, San Diego left no room for defeat, busting the Broncos, 23-0. The Chargers left the field yelling and screaming like high school kids.

"There's a different kind of feeling on this team now," exclaimed Dan Fouts, who became the new starting quarterback. "We feel like we're supposed to win every game. That's a big change from when everyone expected us to lose."

It was no secret that the players believed in themselves. The fans, however, were not as confident. Many of them had turned off their televisions when the Chargers trailed Oakland, 23-14, with still eight minutes remaining. That was too bad, because they missed one of the most exciting comebacks in San Diego history.

Rolf Benirschke, the happy-go-lucky placekicker, started the rally when his field goal cut the lead to 23-17. The Charger defense then rose to the occasion by forcing Oakland to punt. Still, time was growing short.

San Diego got the ball once more with just a minute left. Fouts hit Joiner and Jefferson on back-to-back throws. Then, with only 48 seconds showing on the clock, little-known tight end Greg McCrary found his way free to

Running back Don Woods was drafted and then bounced by Green Bay.
Snapped up by the Chargers in 1974, he became AFC Rookie of the Year.

In 1978, JJ Jefferson caught 56 passes for 1,001 yards and 13 touchdowns.

catch Fouts' last-ditch pass in the end zone. Benirschke then snapped the 23-23 tie by converting the extra point. San Diego had won it!

It was the start of something big. For the next seven weeks, the San Diego Chargers were virtually unbeatable. Cincinnati, Seattle, Kansas City, Minnesota and Houston all fell in the wake of San Diego's late-season charge.

FOUTS AND
AIR CORYELL

When Tommy Prothro drafted Dan Fouts out of Oregon in 1973, people were surprised that he came in the third round. They didn't think Fouts was that good. Oh, sure, he had broken 19 school passing marks at Oregon, but his physical skills were questionable. He was not particularly quick, strong or graceful.

So why did Prothro go after him? "It was just a hunch," he said.

Fouts was anything but an overnight sensation. Injuries sidelined him during his rookie season as he watched Johnny Unitas struggle through the twilight of his career. When Unitas retired, Fouts stepped into the starter's role and gradually showed signs of improvement. Then, when Don Coryell took charge, Fout's career blossomed.

He threw 24 touchdown passes in 1978 as San Diego turned the league upside-down with a blistering airborne attack that the Chargers called "Air Coryell." It was a flat-out, wide-open air circus with the bearded Fouts as its ringmaster. It didn't matter which down it

Did you know?

On January 2,
1982, Rolf Benir-
schke's 27-yard field
goal after 13:52
of overtime gave the
Chargers a dramatic
41-38 victory over
Miami in the
Orange Bowl in one
of the epic games
in NFL history.

might be, or where the ball was placed on the field, the Chargers were going to pass.

In 1979, San Diego captured its first divisional title in 14 years. Give a train-load of credit to Fouts. His total of 4,082 yards through the air shattered one of pro football's most respected records. The old mark of 4,007 had been set by the one-and-only "Broadway Joe" Namath back in 1967. Suddenly, everyone in America knew of Fouts and Air Coryell. Some teams were even copying the San Diego offense.

"But there's no substitute for the real thing, and we have him in Dan Fouts," said Coach Coryell. "Dan has to be one of the most competitive people I know. He's a tremendous leader because he's so mentally tough and determined."

Fouts' teammates called him a perfectionist. "He doesn't tolerate mistakes," explained halfback Chuck Muncie.

While defensive backs dreaded going against him, Fouts' own receivers relished working with him. "When you have a pure passer such as Dan," said split-end Wes Chandler, "for a receiver, it's like you've died and gone to heaven. With Fouts back there, I get real brave."

Another brave player was Benirschke, the San Diego kicker. In 1978, he was on his way to a successful sopho-more season when he developed stomach pains. The pains grew worse, but Benirschke valiantly stayed with the team until his condition became unbearable.

At first, doctors thought he had cancer. Early in 1979, they performed surgery on the young man. Benirschke nearly died because of surgical complications. His weight dropped from 174 to 123 pounds in a matter of days. It

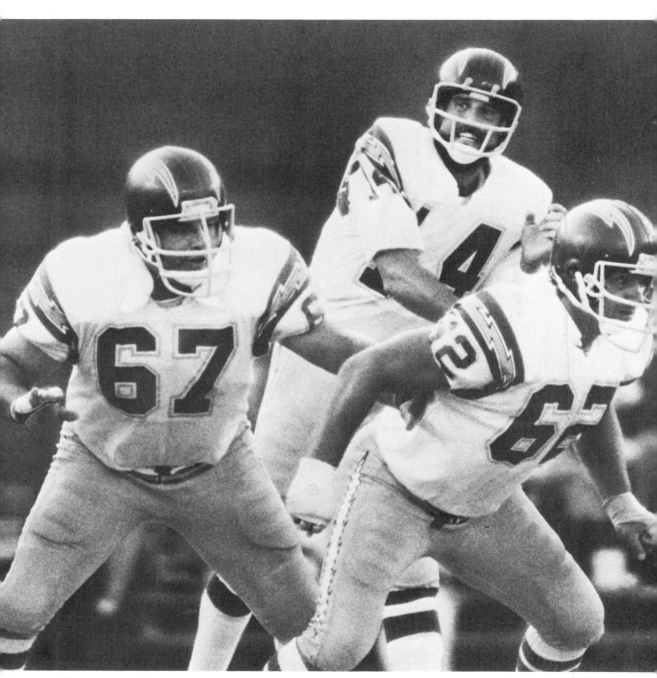

Classic action, Chargers-style! Ed White (67) and Don Macek (62) protect rifle-armed Danny Fouts.

The moving wall: Andrew Gissinger (75) and Dennis McKnight (60) converge on an unfortunate 49er defender in 1984 action.

was nearly a month before he was fit enough to visit his teammates.

The Chargers named him honorary captain for an important game against Pittsburgh. The stadium grew silent as Rolf walked to the center of the field for the coin toss. At first, the fans didn't recognize him. But after a few seconds, they identified those long legs and that warm, friendly smile. Instantly, the crowd erupted in thunderous applause. Spurred on by this touching scene, the Chargers went on to rout the Steelers, 35-7, and by so doing, won the 1979 division crown.

Benirschke's battle was far from over, however. It required months of hard work and rehabilitation for him to regain his weight and strength. But when the 1980 season opened, there was Rolf Benirschke, waiting to kick off.

Did you know?

On November 27, 1983, quarterback John Hadl was inducted into the Chargers' Hall of Fame at halftime of the Denver game.

SAN DIEGO PREPARES TO STRIKE

All systems were go as the 1980 season neared. The Chargers had added a few more rockets to their offensive arsenal during the off-season. One was Kellen Winslow, a young tight end from Missouri, whose built-in homing device was set on "T" for touchdown. Winslow had magnets for hands. Some called him better than All-Pro. Scouts labeled him "All-World."

Then, in a surprising trade with New Orleans, Coryell had walked off with Chuck Muncie, a thousand-yard runner who was also a great receiver.

Like a time bomb whose hour had come, San Diego exploded in 1980, winning its first five games in succession. The mighty "Air Coryell" offense ascended to new heights with each passing game.

Winslow captured nationwide attention when he almost single-handedly beat the Raiders, catching 12 passes and scoring three touchdowns in a dramatic, 30-24, overtime win.

Some quarterbacks pick apart defenses. But the next week against the New York Giants, Fouts rudely ripped gaping holes in the Giants' game plan, passing for a club record 444 yards and three TD's as the Chargers won in a rout, 44-7. Two weeks later, it was Muncie's turn. He ran wild against Denver, gaining 115 yards on the ground, and many more through the air.

On the final day of the regular season, a Monday night game against Pittsburgh, San Diego blew open the contest in the fourth quarter with two scoring strikes from Fouts. The fans danced in the aisles of San Diego's Jack Murphy Stadium, and for good reason. This was more than just another win; the Chargers had just clinched the 1980 Western Division title.

Unlike the year before, San Diego with its 11-5 record simply dispensed with Buffalo in the first round of the '80 playoffs. The Super Bowl was just one step away. The only remaining obstacle was the rival Raiders.

The Chargers fought gallantly, twice taking the lead, but Oakland was not to be denied. Jim Plunkett rallied his troops and overtook San Diego in the final minutes for a 34-27 win, snipping the Chargers' championship hopes. Back to the drawing boards for Air Coryell.

Tight-end Eric Sievers seldom sees his name in the headlines, but his fellow Chargers consider him to be the hardest worker on the team.

In '85, Charlie Joiner headed into his seventeenth NFL season, intent on securing his place as the most productive receiver in the history of pro football.

THIS IS IT!

Many experts suggested that there was little room for improvement in the Chargers' passing attack. It was too good, too complete. Don Coryell disagreed.

"There's always room for another outstanding player," he said. But to make room, the Chargers had to release the great John Jefferson. Only a few receivers rated better than JJ, but Wes Chandler—the All-Pro end from New Orleans—was one of them.

Chandler jumped up and down when he heard about the trade. "The offense in San Diego is grrrrreat," he exclaimed. "It's designed to let all the players use their talents to the fullest. I have certain vibes. It's a vibe that says, 'Hey this is going to be it.'"

In 1981, Fouts' pass-happy offense took right off where it had ended the year before. Danny hit for 330 yards through the airways in a smashing 44-14 opening-night victory over Cleveland. Muncie ran for 161 more and Charlie Joiner, not to be out-done by Chandler and Winslow, caught eight passes for 191 yards.

Once again, San Diego raced to the division crown with a 10-6 mark. But the task ahead was not easy. The determined Miami Dolphins held the home-field advantage in the first round of the 1981 playoffs. Nothing could stop the high-scoring crew of Air Coryell, however. Fouts shredded the Dolphins' defensive secondary for a playoff record 433 yards passing.

Winslow was all over the field that day. He latched onto 13 passes for 122 yards. He scored a touchdown. His blocks paved the way for a series of end sweeps by Muncie. Twice, Winslow had to be helped from the

How running back Chuck Muncie described Chargers guard Doug Wilkerson: "Doug is like a fine Cadillac—he gives me fingertip control. I don't have to read him. I never have to hesitate behind him. Moose is like another pair of eyes."

field after taking big hits from Miami tacklers.

Then, with only :04 showing on the clock, Winslow trotted onto the field to take his revenge. Lining up as defensive end, he broke through to block a Miami field-goal attempt, sending the game into overtime at 38-38. From there on, Fouts went to work, passing to Chandler and Joiner to set up Rolf Benirschke's game-winning field goal. Thank you, Mr. Benirsche. And a special thanks to Kellen Winslow for making that kick possible.

Once more, San Diego stood just one step away from its goal, the Super Bowl. This time the Chargers' opponent in the AFC Championship game was the Cincinnati Bengals. All during the week prior to the game, the Chargers practiced diligently in 70-degree heat. Only one problem—the game was being played in Cincinnati, and the entire Ohio Valley was frozen solid.

Fouts and Air Coryell never got off the ground in the minus-9-degree (-59 with wind-chill factor) Cincinnati deep-freeze. Winslow thawed out enough to grab one scoring pass, but the Bengals won easily, 27-7.

"I can't tell you how much it hurts to come this far and lose two years in a row," said Coryell after the loss. San Diego fans shared his grief.

GOOD NEWS
ON THE
HORIZON

The next three seasons were hard on the San Diego Chargers. Defensive mainstays Fred Dean, Louie Kelcher and Gary Johnson left the club. Chuck Muncie was sus-

In 1983, Rolf Benirschke turned in a season that made him the most accurate kicker in NFL history with an astounding .720 field-goal percentage!

pended for breaking team drug rules. Winslow ("Oh no, not Winslow," groaned the fans.) was lost to knee surgery. Even Dan Fouts was in and out of the lineup with shoulder injuries.

San Diego limped and gimped its way to a 6-3 record in 1982, 6-10 in 1983, and 7-9 in 1984. But there was good news on the horizon.

Fouts, who had been slowed by assorted ailments for a number of years, looked fit and healthy as the 1985 season neared. Charlie Joiner—who became the NFL's most prolific pass-catcher in 1984—and Chandler were also back in action. Oh yes, and a young halfback named Earnest T. Jackson had established himself as one of the NFL's most promising stars.

Once again, it appears Air Coryell is cleared for take-off. It's destination? Super Bowl, USA.

Heading into the 1985 season, Coach Coryell slung his arm around Dan Fout's shoulder and put it this way: "You aren't a champion team until you've won the Super Bowl. I want that to happen. Dan Fouts wants that to happen. The Chargers and their great fans want that to happen. Now, let's see that it does."

He was great in '83, '84 and '85, but nothing could top Wes Chandler's '82 performance when he overcame five separate injuries to turn in the most productive single season of any receiver in NFL history.